Europe in 1360

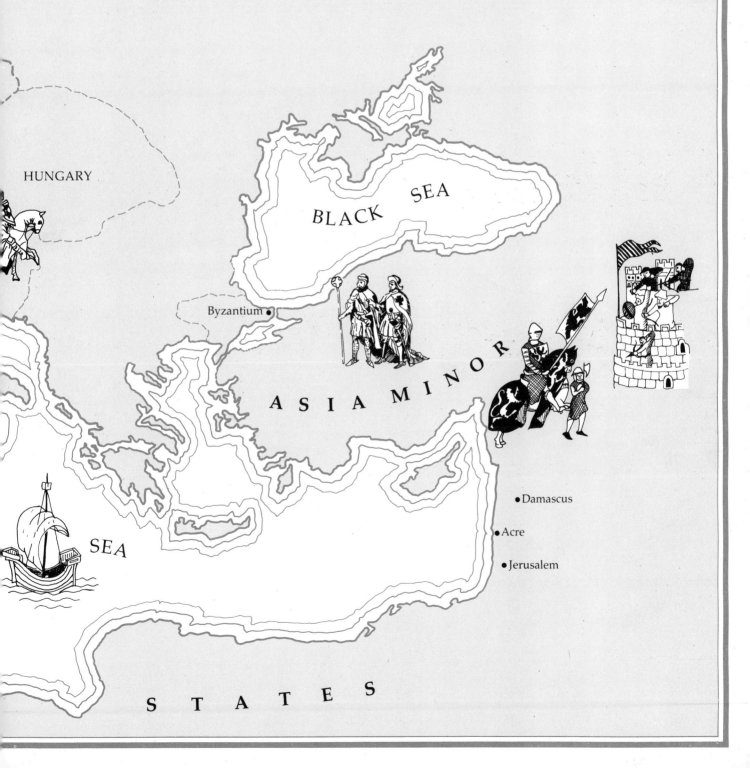

HUNGARY

BLACK SEA

Byzantium •

A S I A M I N O R

SEA

• Damascus

• Acre

• Jerusalem

S T A T E S

I WAS THERE
KNIGHTS
IN ARMOUR

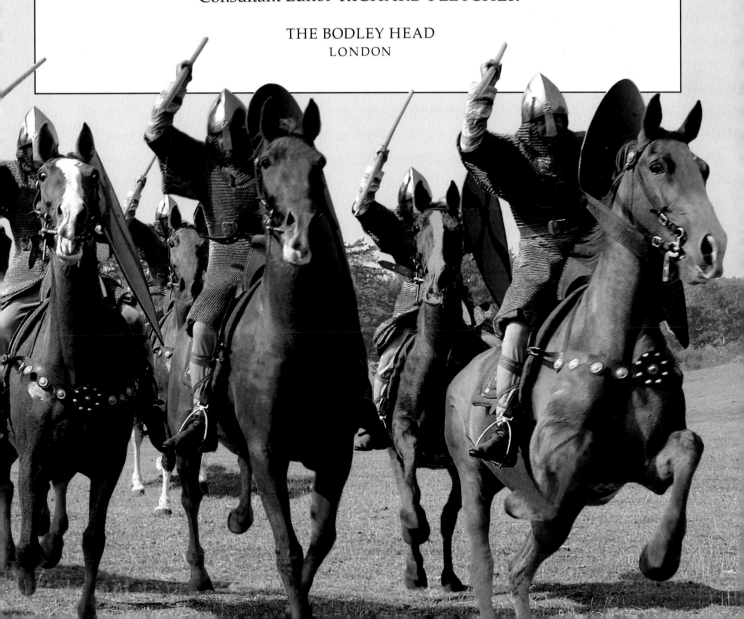

I WAS THERE

KNIGHTS
IN ARMOUR

JOHN D. CLARE

Consultant Editor RICHARD FLETCHER

THE BODLEY HEAD
LONDON

First published in Great Britain in 1991
by The Bodley Head Children's Books,
an imprint of The Random Century Group Ltd
20 Vauxhall Bridge Road, London SW1V 2SA

Random Century Australia Pty Ltd
20 Alfred Street, Sydney, NSW 2061

Random Century New Zealand Ltd
PO Box 40-086, Glenfield, Auckland 10, New Zealand

Random Century South Africa Pty Ltd
PO Box 337, Bergvlei 2012, South Africa

ISBN   0-370-31660-6

A CIP catalogue record for this book is available from
the British Library

Created and produced by Roxby Paintbox Co. Ltd
126 Victoria Rise, London SW4 0NW

Director of Photography Tymn Lyntell
Photography Charles Best
Second Unit Photography Roger di Vito
Art Director Dalia Hartman
Production Manager Fiona Nicholson
Visualisation/Systems Operator Antony Parks

Editor Gilly Abrahams
Consultant Editor Richard Fletcher
Series Editor Susan Elwes
Editorial Assistant Valerie Tongue
Map/Time-line Simon Ray-Hills
Typesetting Sue Estermann

Reproduction F. E. Burman Ltd, Columbia Offset Ltd,
Dalim Computer Graphic Systems U.K. Ltd,
J. Film Process Ltd, Trademasters Ltd

Printed by Arti Grafiche Motta S.p.A., Milan, Italy

ACKNOWLEDGEMENTS

Costumes: Val Metheringham, Joanna Measure. Make-
up: Alex Cawdron, Louise Fisher, Caroline Kelly, Sarah
Packham, Jan Harrison Shell. Models: Chris Lovell,
Neville Smith. Props: Caroline Gardener, Mark Roberts.
Period consultant, fight director and casting: Mike
Loades assisted by Gordon Summers. Photographer's
assistant: Alex Rhodes. Picture research: Valerie Tongue.

Roxby Paintbox would also like to thank the following:
Denny Edwards, Berman's International; the Henson
family, Cotswold Farm Park; Andy Deane; Tom Brumby,
English Heritage; The Free Companies, Colchester;
Tim and Jennifer Hulme, Canterbury; Roy King; Ken
Measday; Jeremy Goldsmith, Mount Fitchett Castle;
The Rare Breeds Survival Trust Ltd; Tom Richardson,
The Royal Armouries; The Royal Shakespeare Company;
Singleton Open Air Museum; 1471 Society; John
Thompson; The Tower of London; John Waller;
Jonathan Waller; Pam and Paul Brown of Zara Training
Centre, Sidlesham.

Additional photographs: Reproduced by Courtesy of
The Trustees of The British Museum, p63 top left; Glasgow
University Library, p62 left; Michael Boys/Susan Griggs
Agency, pp58-9; Antony Parks, pp24-5, 28-9, 34-5; Public
Record Office, p62 right (DL 10/38); Ronald Sheridan's
Photo-Library, p6 top and bottom; Zefa Picture Library,
pp26-7, 44-5, 56-7.

Contents

The Coming of the Knight 6

The Development of Armour 8

The Royal Progress 11

The Feudal System 13

In the Pillory 14

Paying Tithes 16

On Pilgrimage 18

Crusade! 20

The First Crusade 22

Defeat of the Crusades 24

A Woman's Role 27

Women in the Solar 28

Page and Squire 30

Accolade 32

Knight Errantry 34

Chivalry 37

Making Armour 38

Arming the Knight 40

Weapons and White Armour 42

The Siege 45

Starving out the Enemy 47

Fighting on Horseback 48

The Darker Side of War 50

The Chase 52

The Tournament 54

The Professional Soldier 56

Gunpowder 58

The New Knights 60

How Do We Know? 62

Index 64

The Coming of the Knight

The age of the knight began in about AD 900 and lasted until around 1500, the end of the period historians call the Middle Ages. These were hard times. Ordinary people were so poor they had to share their single-roomed huts with their animals. At night they sat on roughly made furniture amongst rotting food scraps and manure, their eyes smarting from the fire smoke. Famines, and epidemics such as the Black Death, were frequent. Most people died before the age of 30.

Without the calming influence of older, wiser advisers, rulers were often foolish and violent. City authorities would build a stage in the marketplace so that the inhabitants could watch criminals being tortured. For entertainment, blind beggars would be forced to beat a pig to death, while clumsily hitting each other in the confusion.

The divisions of society

Medieval society was divided into three groups: the clergy, the workers and the warriors.

The raids of the Vikings in the ninth century had almost destroyed the Church. A Council of Bishops held near Soissons in France in AD 909 complained that the abbeys had been demolished and the Christian customs forgotten. During the Middle Ages, however, the Church regained its power. Many new monasteries were built and a strict regime was imposed on the monks. The Church developed canon law (rules laying down what a Christian had to believe) and a court system called the Inquisition to discover and punish heretics (people who disagreed with its teachings). In the Middle Ages you would be denounced as a heretic if you believed that the earth travelled round the sun or doubted the story of creation in the Bible.

Christianity – and Latin, which was spoken by all learned people – became the unifying force of medieval Europe. Most people in western Europe were Roman Catholics and accepted the Pope as their spiritual leader.

The majority of the workers in medieval society were villeins (peasants), who worked

in the fields. The rest were craftsmen or tradesmen who lived in the towns.

There were few large towns in the Middle Ages; only a dozen in the whole of Europe had over 100,000 inhabitants. The Church said that towns were 'accursed' places and used the Bible as proof: Cain, the murderer, had built a town, but Abraham had built an altar. Church leaders forbade moneylending or trading for profit and condemned many trades as 'contemptible professions' because, it was said, they encouraged the seven deadly sins. Merchants and cooks were greedy;

innkeepers and cloth-makers encouraged lust. Other tradesmen condemned by the Church included doctors, gardeners, pastry-makers, cobblers and tripe-sellers. Even beggars were criticized – they were guilty of laziness.

As the Middle Ages continued, towns and trade expanded. Craftsmen banded together into groups called guilds, to control their industry and maintain standards. The none (noon) bell was changed from its original time of 2 p.m. to 12 a.m., to reduce workers' lunchtime, it has been suggested. Some craftsmen tried to strike about the hours of work, but they were told that the working day was 'from the hour of sunrise to the hour of sunset'. Italian towns such as Venice began to trade with the Middle East, Persia and India. Marco Polo travelled to China. The missionary knight Raimon Llull journeyed into the Sahara, where he met a caravan of 6,000 camels laden with salt.

The wars of the Middle Ages, however, frequently harmed trade. Contact with Muslim Africa and the East became more and more difficult. In the west, Greenland and America, discovered by the Vikings, were forgotten. Medieval technology remained backward. Science was dominated by the ideas of ancient writers such as the Greeks. Medicine, which had been advanced by the Greeks and Romans, slid back into superstition – it was believed that a dog's lick would heal a snakebite, and that saying the Lord's Prayer cured toothache. In their laboratories, medieval alchemists tried to turn lead into gold and to discover 'the fountain of all health'.

The warrior class

Most of Europe was divided into small states, each ruled by a duke or a count who was supposed to obey his king or emperor, although in practice he did as he pleased. One state was ruled by the Pope. The states of Europe were constantly at war, and it was in this world of wars that knighthood developed.

At first the knight was simply a cavalry soldier. The French word for knight (*chevalier*) means a horseman. A warhorse and armour, however, were very expensive, so a king had to ensure that his knights had enough land to bring in a good income. Gradually, the knights acquired certain legal and government duties. People wanted to be knighted because it gave them power and respectability. In time, all nobles became knights. Even kings had their sons knighted.

In France and Spain all knights were nobles, whether they were rich or poor. In England, confusingly, knight also came to mean a person in the third rank of society, after the king and the nobles.

A knight was expected to be gallant and brave, gentle and bold. The ideal knight rode on a white charger to defend the poor and rescue damsels in distress. This way of behaving was called chivalry.

Many knights, however, did not live up to these high standards. In the early days they were often ignorant and barbaric. Invading soldiers threw babies into the air and caught them on their spears. One French knight, Bernard de Cahuzac, cut off the hands and feet of 150 monks and nuns after a disagreement with the local abbot.

The Development of Armour

Although it is often thought that society made no progress during the Middle Ages, in warfare, at least, there was an arms race. New weapons were constantly being invented, which led to new developments in armour.

In the eleventh and twelfth centuries the knight wore a hauberk (coat of mail), usually made from interlinking rings. Another type of hauberk was made from small pieces of metal riveted to a leather tunic (scale armour). Under this the knight wore a padded jacket called an aketon, which absorbed the impact of blows from enemy weapons. Mail armour weighed over 30 pounds (13.5 kilograms). In direct sunlight it became excessively hot, so the knight often put a surcoat (light tunic) over his hauberk to deflect the sun's rays.

During the thirteenth and fourteenth centuries knights started wearing steel plate extensions to protect the more vulnerable parts of the body. A heavy metal helm (helmet) covered the head. The infantry soldiers of the time said that the only way to kill a knight was to knock him to the ground and beat him to death.

In the fifteenth century complete plate armour was developed.

Left to right: how armour developed. The twelfth-century knight wears mail armour. The mail mittens, which have leather palms, are called mufflers; mail chausses (trousers) protect the legs and feet; a mail coif protects the shoulders; the red aketon shows through beneath the surcoat. The helm bears the knight's heraldic crest.

By the fourteenth century plate covers the vulnerable parts of the body. Pauldrons, couters, gauntlets, cuisses and poleyns cover the shoulders, elbows, hands, thighs and knees. A mail skirt is still worn and a mail collar is attached to the bascinet (helmet), with its hounskull (pig-faced) vizor, which can be raised for a breath of air.

By the late fifteenth century plate armour has been perfected and it is possible to cover the knight completely (see page 42).

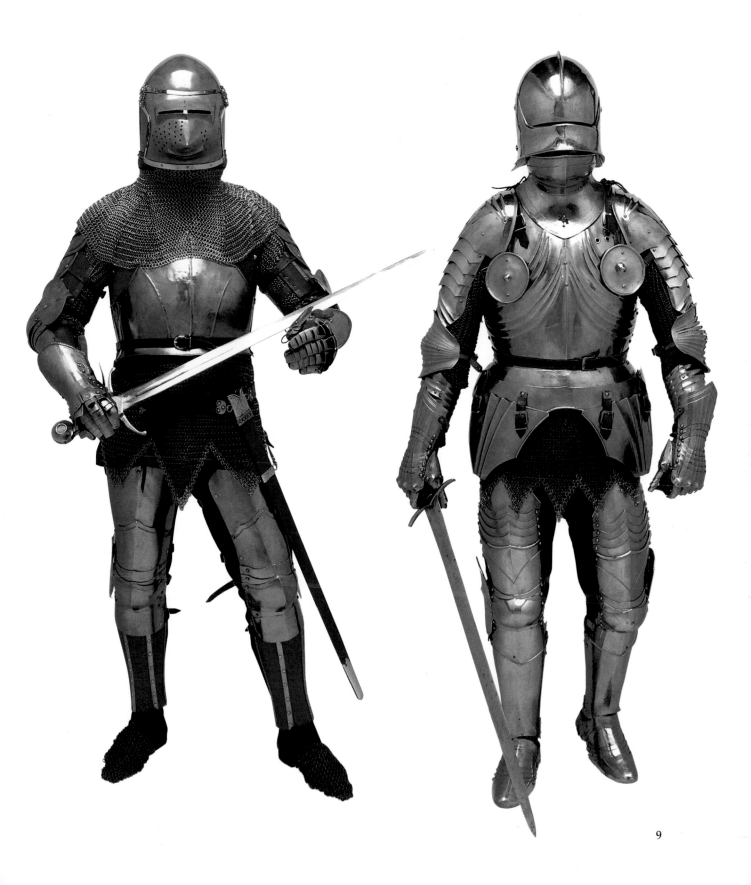

The Royal Progress

A king had to rule over his people. He had to defend the country, make laws and frighten criminals with terrible punishments. Medieval kings were also thought to be able to heal the sick. The disease known today as scrofula was called the king's evil, because a king's touch was supposed to cure it. People rebelled if a king was too weak to do these things.

At his coronation a king received a sword and a crown – symbols of his power and authority. He was anointed with holy oil and became 'king by the grace of God'. Some of the prayers and ceremonies still survive in the British coronation service.

Protected by his knights, a king and his royal court travelled continually round the kingdom, to make sure that the nobles and judges were keeping the king's laws. Travelling with the king were his chamberlains, stewards, treasurers, clerks and chaplains. In the early Middle Ages, wives were left at home.

Henry II of England (1154-89) rarely rested and his legs were always sore from so much riding. He would wake up in the middle of the night and decide to move on. 'Immediately everywhere is confusion,' wrote one eye-witness. 'Men run about like mad, waggons crash into each other, and pack horses are quickly loaded.'

The servants – cooks, butlers, grooms, valets, fools (jesters) and washerwomen – follow immediately behind the main court. With them travel members of the public who wish to bring their legal cases directly to the king.

Accidents are common on the poorly maintained roads. The women call for help to right the cart, because stragglers frequently fall prey to outlaws, robbers and murderers.

The Feudal System

A knight's horse and armour cost a great deal – the equivalent of 23 cows – and in the early Middle Ages the king could not afford to finance even a small cavalry force. Instead, he granted fiefs (estates) to his barons if they promised to provide a certain number of knights for his army. In times of trouble the king would proclaim the *arrière-ban* (call to arms). In England, in 1205, the cavalry comprised about 5,000 knights.

Sometimes other duties were added to the 'rent'. Henry de la Wade, who was granted 500 acres (202 hectares), had to supply the king with falcons for hawking. Rowland le Sarcere held 110 acres (45 hectares) on the understanding that every Christmas he would perform before the king 'a jump, a puff and a rude noise'.

The barons rented their lands to others, in return for goods and services. A baron would grant a manor to a knight who promised to fight for him in the event of war. A blacksmith might be given 4 acres (1.5 hectares) and a smithy in return for shoeing the baron's horses and mending the ploughs.

Any man (even a nobleman) who rented land was called a vassal and had to make an oath of allegiance (loyalty) to his lord. Kneeling down, he placed both hands between those of the lord and said, 'I become your man from this day forward, and unto you shall be true and faithful for the lands I hold from you.'

Villeins, who are the lowest class of society, are given a small plot of land. In return they work for their lord (above) or give him a proportion of their produce.

It is vital for everyone, including the knight, that the harvest is successful. If the village fields do not produce a good crop, many people will starve to death – there is no other way of obtaining food.

The villeins' lives are full of toil and danger. When new land is brought into cultivation, the soil has to be broken up with a hoe (main picture). Shepherds (above, top) have to protect their flocks against wolves and bears.

In the Pillory

When a knight was granted land by the king or a baron, he became lord of the manor and was entitled to receive goods and services from the villeins who lived on the estate. In one typical village each villein held 30 acres (12 hectares). In return he had to work two days a week on the lord's land, put in extra hours at harvest time, guard the castle and wait at the lord's table at Christmas. In addition, each year he had to give the lord 48 bags of malt, 16 bags of grain, eight cartloads of wood, 30 hens and a thousand eggs. It left little for his family.

Sometimes humiliating services were added to these duties. In one French village the peasants had to kiss the door of the manor house. In another, they had to stay up all night beating the village pond, to prevent the frogs from croaking and waking the lord.

A villein paid a relief when he took up a tenancy, and a merchet when his daughter married. In some villages the lord could stay with the girl on her wedding night. A heriot payment (the best animal and sometimes all

the furniture) had to be handed over to the lord when a villein died. By law the villeins were the knight's property and were sold along with the land.

At regular intervals the lord of the manor held a court baron, to deal with the minor problems of village life. At the court, villagers would be given punishments if it was proved that they had, for example, chopped down the lord's trees, grazed cattle on his land or attacked their neighbours. If the lord failed to exercise his rights, the peasants became the owners of their land.

Some knights thought that 'villeins, like trees, grow better if they are cut back'. They plundered the villages and tortured the peasants, crushing them in shallow chests lined with nails and sharp stones. The wife of the French knight Bernard de Cahuzac enjoyed pulling out the fingernails of peasant girls, so that they could not work.

The villein in the pillory is a troublesome man who regularly appears before the manor court. This time he has seized a pig and attacked the village bailiff, who looks after the lord's property. He will be kept in the pillory all day so that the villagers can hurl abuse at him and bombard him with vegetables and stones.

Paying Tithes

In the Middle Ages people believed that if they were wicked 'the devils would seize them and carry them away to hell' when they died. Even good people expected to spend thousands of years in purgatory (which was not quite as bad as hell) before they could go to heaven.

The Church claimed to be able to control these matters. It could grant an indulgence to reduce a person's time in purgatory, or it could excommunicate them and refuse Christian burial, thereby sending them to hell.

Most of Europe was Christian so the Church had great authority, even over kings. In 1076 Pope Gregory VII excommunicated the Holy Roman Emperor, Henry IV. Henry had to cross the Alps in midwinter, to beg the Pope's forgiveness.

The Church also used its influence to try to control the behaviour of the knights. In 1041 a Church council in France proclaimed the Truce of God, forbidding soldiers to fight on Sundays or holy days. The proper tasks of a knight, it said, were to defend the Church and the poor, and to fight against evil.

These ideas had a great effect on the knights. Many had younger brothers who had gone into the priesthood to make a living, as only the eldest son inherited family land.

A monk collects the priest's tithes (tenths) from the villagers. He demands a tenth of everything – crops, fruit, hay, livestock and milk. Merchants and craftsmen pay a tenth of their profits.

People hate paying the tithe to the priest, because he keeps it all for himself and lives in luxury. Some farmers take the milk tithe to the church in large buckets. If they find no-one present, they pour the milk onto the floor in front of the altar.

On Pilgrimage

Knights lived by breaking the sixth commandment ('Thou shalt not kill'), so they sometimes tried to earn God's forgiveness by going on a pilgrimage to a holy place. Fulk the Black, a French nobleman who had massacred his enemies and murdered his wife, made three pilgrimages to Jerusalem where he did penance for his sins. While monks beat him with branches, he shouted: 'Accept, O Lord, the wretched Fulk.'

Ordinary people went on pilgrimage in the hope of being healed at a holy place, or to see the sights. In Rome a pilgrim might see an altar built by St Peter, a self-portrait of the Virgin Mary, the table used for the Last Supper, and the napkin which had covered the face of Jesus. People who had visited Rome wore a small napkin as a badge and were called Romers (hence the verb to roam). Compostela pilgrims wore a seashell and people who had been to Jerusalem (palmers) wore a palm leaf.

Pilgrims – like those in Chaucer's *Canterbury Tales* – travelled in groups, with the thieves and murderers who were going on a pilgrimage instead of going to prison. They carried travel guides telling them what to take and where to stay.

The Society of the Knights Templars was formed in 1118 to protect pilgrims who came to the Holy Land. Pilgrims could pay money into Templar castles in the West, and draw it out when they reached Jerusalem. The Templars arranged transport and accommodation, and trips to places of interest – the first package holidays.

Pilgrims pause on their way to the shrine of St James of Compostela in Spain. It is the busiest road in Europe. Along the way dozens of fake shrines have been set up to attract passers-by.

Crusade!

Since AD 638 Jerusalem, the most important city in the Christian faith, had been controlled by Muslims. In 1009 they had destroyed the Church of the Holy Sepulchre in Jerusalem. Pilgrims to the Holy Land were attacked. Hundreds were killed in 1064 when a party of 12,000 pilgrims was ambushed. Many people wanted Jerusalem to be recaptured by a Christian army.

There were other pressures for a military crusade (expedition). The Church thought that a holy war would keep the violent knights usefully occupied. Also, the younger sons of noblemen hoped to win wealth and glory. There were 'signs', too, which convinced people that God wanted a crusade. It was said that stars had fallen from heaven and

that children had been born with extra limbs. A priest claimed that he had seen a crusader and a Saracen (a Muslim) fighting in the air.

At this time the Roman Catholic Church was divided, with two men claiming to be the true pope. One of them, Urban II, realized that organizing a crusade would give him an advantage over his rival.

At the end of the eleventh century the Muslim armies attacked the Byzantine Empire in eastern Europe. The emperor sent his ambassadors to Italy to ask for help. It was the excuse Urban needed to call for a crusade.

It is 27 November 1095. Pope Urban has summoned France's leading churchmen to meet him in Clermont. He blesses them and tells them to spread the idea of a holy war. Jerusalem, he says, is held captive by God's enemies, and he lists Muslim atrocities. 'Who will avenge all this, who will repair the damage?' he asks. 'God wills that we should do it,' the people reply.

The First Crusade

In 1095 Urban travelled round Europe for eight months, encouraging people to go on crusade to free the Holy Land. In Germany some peasants became so enthusiastic they set off immediately. They were led by Peter the Hermit, a preacher, and Walter the Penniless, a poor knight. They fought their way through Hungary, looting and burning as they went. When they reached Asia Minor (now part of Turkey) they were ambushed and killed.

Some months later the main army of about 4,000 knights and 26,000 footsoldiers set out from Byzantium. After a three-year campaign they captured Jerusalem on 15 July 1099. According to one eyewitness, they slaughtered the Muslims until they 'waded in blood up to their ankles', then they seized all the gold, silver and horses. Finally, they went to worship at the tomb of Christ. The order of events gives some indication of the crusaders' priorities.

Not all the crusaders were bloodthirsty thieves. A few were genuinely religious. They joined Orders of Chivalry, such as the Templars and the Hospitallers, and promised to live in poverty and to remain unmarried. They frowned upon worldly pastimes such as chess,

singing and feasting. One Templar, nicknamed Sir Bread-and-Water, was so weakened from fasting that he fell from his horse as soon as he was hit in battle.

Although some wealthy crusaders travel in comfort with their entire household, this poor French knight takes only his squire, two horses, weapons, clothing and the most basic equipment. He leaves his wife to manage the tiny fief with the help of a few old servants.

The knight has confessed his sins, taken Communion and received the Church's blessing. Now he goes 'to break heads and arms, to hear the cries of "At them!", to kill the heathen' – and, perhaps, to win his fortune.

Defeat of the Crusades

During the next two hundred years six more crusades were launched to defend the Kingdom of Jerusalem established by the First Crusade in 1099.

The conflict was bitter and vicious. When the Second Crusade marched on Damascus in 1148, the Muslims ambushed them in an orchard, stabbing them with lances through peepholes in the walls. Christians on the Third Crusade ate the flesh of murdered Muslim hostages, and Richard the Lionheart hung Saracens' heads from his saddle. After the capture of one town, the crusaders executed 2,700 prisoners, ripping open the corpses to find any jewels that the Muslims had swallowed in an attempt to hide them.

The crusaders' desire for glory continually brought disaster. At the Battle of Cresson (1187) the Templars' Grand Master taunted a

band of knights until they attacked the main Muslim army. Only three knights survived. The Kingdom of Jerusalem, with an army of 1,500 knights at most, lost a hundred men in one foolish charge.

Many crusaders quarrelled and plotted against each other, and were more interested in plunder than in battle. The Fourth Crusade, instead of attacking the Muslims, looted Byzantium, the city they were supposed to be defending. Too few in number, the crusaders could not resist the Muslim armies for ever. Jerusalem was captured in 1244. The city of Acre, the last crusader stronghold in the Holy Land, fell in 1291. The crusades had failed.

Unable to defeat the heavily armed crusaders in battle, the Muslim soldiers mount surprise attacks on supply convoys and stragglers. Here, a party of lightly armed Muslim horsemen ambushes a small scouting party of crusaders.

A Woman's Role

Some women were remarkably successful in the man's world of the Middle Ages. In the twelfth century Eleanor of Aquitaine, who went on crusade in full armour, organized a rebellion against her husband, King Henry II of England. Christine de Pisan, a Frenchwoman who married at 15 and became a widow at 25, made her living as a writer.

Although few women fought in battle like Joan of Arc, they often had to organize the defence of a castle. The Countess of Buchan defended Berwick Castle so fiercely against King Edward I of England that when he finally over-came her soldiers he hung her over the battlements in an iron cage. In 1341 the Countess of Brittany not only defended her husband's castle but led a counter-attack with 'the courage of a man and the bravery of a lion'.

Women could not be knighted but they could become honorary members of certain knightly orders, such as the Order of St John of Jerusalem. In France an Order of Cordeliers was created solely for widows.

A knight's wife looked after the children and organized all the domestic tasks such as cooking, brewing, making clothes and pick-ing lice and fleas out of everyone's hair. However, she also hired the labourers, supervised the stewards, sold the produce and kept the accounts.

The Middle Ages were violent times and men often died before their wives. It was common, therefore, for a woman to find her-self managing an estate, either in her own right or on behalf of a young son.

Expecting attack while her husband is away, a noble-woman directs the building of hoardings, from which boiling oil can be poured if the castle is assaulted.

Women in the Solar

Although women had many responsibilities, and a few gained power and fame, in general they were not regarded as equal with men in the Middle Ages. Church leaders argued that women were evil. Had not Eve eaten the apple and caused Adam to sin? Woman, they said, 'is of feeble kind, and makes more lies'.

The law let a man beat his wife if he thought she was at fault – for instance, if she had borne him a mentally handicapped child. It was believed that the four sayings of the Virgin Mary recorded in the Bible were *all* that Mary had said in her entire life. Medieval ladies were advised to keep as quiet, and to devote themselves to their domestic jobs – 'like slaves or prisoners' one wife complained.

Girls were used by their parents to secure social and political advantage through

marriage. Gracia, daughter of Thomas de Sakeby, an English nobleman, was married in 1198 to Adam de Neville. She was four years old. Before she was 11 she had been widowed twice and had married again. In 1449, 20-year-old Elizabeth Paston was beaten twice a day by her mother for refusing to marry a 50-year-old widower permanently disfigured by illness.

A girl was taught to obey her husband. She had no privacy; doors were left open. In a small household the wife often had to choose between unbearable loneliness or the shame of mixing with the serving girls.

The lord's wife and her ladies-in-waiting have retired to the solar (the ladies' room). This is their women-only world where they are able to cultivate a more refined society. They embroider, make music, play chess and read stories of love and chivalry. Men are only admitted to talk to the ladies if they can prove that they are educated, polite and witty.

Page and Squire

When a boy was born into a noble household, the rumour (news of the birth) was rushed to the father. The bearer of the good news was rewarded. If the mother was too young to look after the baby herself – many young wives gave birth in their early teens – the family employed a nurse.

Boys' games taught them how to behave like knights. One game was called 'robber baron', and another 'the king doesn't lie'. The boys made hobbyhorses and showed off to the girls by charging at each other.

At seven, the son of a knight was taken to another nobleman's household to be trained as a page. He spent the next seven years learning weapon skills, as well as riding, hunting and hawking, chess, music and dancing. He was taught to love God. He also served at table, to learn that the highest honour was to serve others.

A noblewoman in the household became the page's special friend, so he could learn how to treat a lady. In later times, he was taught above all to behave properly. 'Do not scratch your head, nor spit too far.... Do not sigh, or belch, or with puffing and blowing cast foul breath upon your lord,' advised the fifteenth-century *Babies' Book of Nurture*, a book of rules for pages.

At 14 the page became a squire. He was given a sword and belt in a short church ceremony and for the next seven years trained for battle and the joust (see page 54). He still served at meals, but did the more important jobs such as pouring the wine or carving the meat. The Squire of the Honours stood by his lord's chair, carried his helmet and banner, led his horse and raised his battle cry.

A page serves at table (left), while the squire (main picture) fights with staves, hawks, practises archery and learns to charge, using a quintain as his target. A high-born squire also plays the rebec (below).

Accolade

In theory, a squire would become a knight at the age of 21. However, those who were too poor to buy their own equipment remained squires all their lives.

A rich nobleman's son, on the other hand, might be knighted when he was only 12 years old. A knight was a soldier in the army, but knighthood was also a grade of society and wealthy people did not want their children to remain mere squires.

People believed that knighthood, like the priesthood, was a holy calling. The knighting ceremony, therefore, was a religious occasion. With his companions, the young man spent most of the night in prayer. He was given a bath, symbolizing the washing away of his sins. He lay on a bed to dry, to remind him of the rest that God would give his brave knights in heaven. In the morning he was dressed in a white shirt, a gold tunic and a purple cloak, and was knighted by the king.

Later in the Middle Ages the ceremony became very elaborate. The young man's sword was blessed. He vowed to obey the rules of chivalry and never to run away in battle. The king dubbed him on the neck with the flat of his sword. Then ladies buckled on his armour, starting with the spurs – the symbol of courage.

Squires might also be knighted before a battle, to give them courage. On one occasion the English Earl of Suffolk knighted a French soldier who had captured him – he was too proud to allow himself to be captured by a mere squire!

This squire has won his spurs by showing courage in battle. On the field, the ceremony is brief. The lord simply hits the man hard on his shoulder and says, 'Be thou a knight.' The blow, with the sword or the fist, is called the accolade. The knight will remember this moment for the rest of his life.

Knight Errantry

During the twelfth century two kinds of heroic story became popular. The *chansons de geste* were songs about the deeds of the great Emperor Charlemagne. The romances were stories about King Arthur, a legendary sixth-century king who ruled England with his Knights of the Round Table. In these tales the heroes were knights errant. They put green tunics over their armour and green covers over their shields, then rode out to fight dragons, rescue damsels and find the Holy Grail (the cup used at the Last Supper).

Many medieval knights heard the stories and decided that they too would become knights errant. They travelled round Europe, fighting for good causes, behaving nobly and wearing their ladies' colours.

Other knights had more practical reasons for going on their travels. A knight needed at least three horses, armour, and the services of a squire, costing hundreds of pounds. He was expected to show largesse (generosity) and be extravagant – one twelfth-century knight sowed a field with 30,000 silver coins. Knights who were not very wealthy had to travel round the tournaments, in the hope of making a living from prize money. Successful knights were the popular heroes of their day. The thirteenth-century jouster Ulrich von Lichtenstein toured Italy, Austria and Germany.

During tournaments he dressed as Frau Venus, and promised to give all his horses to any knight who defeated him. The knights he defeated had to bow down in honour of Ulrich's lady.

A young knight passes through a village on the way to the next tournament. His squire follows with the booty he won in his last melee (a fight between teams of knights), when he captured and ransomed a number of wealthy knights.

Chivalry

In 1265 a Spanish knight, Raimon Llull, wrote that knights must be chivalrous – truthful, kind to the poor, loyal and courteous, even in war.

The Law of Arms laid down how they had to behave in battle. They could not mistreat captives or leave an enemy knight to die of his wounds. At the Battle of Poitiers (1356), King Jean of France postponed his attack to avoid fighting on a Sunday. The delay, which allowed the English to prepare, cost him the victory.

During the twelfth century some knights became jongleurs (minstrels). Influenced by their songs of chivalry and love, many knights gave their hearts to young ladies. It did not matter if the lady was married; in the Middle Ages marriage was a business arrangement. True love was the hopeless longing for someone you could never marry.

This courtly love was one of the strangest aspects of chivalry. Knights did great feats just to win a smile. One knight fought in a tournament wearing his lady's dress instead of his armour. He was badly wounded. The lady's husband gave a feast in the knight's honour and the lady wore the blood-stained dress. Harsh words were exchanged before the Battle of Poitiers when Sir John Chandos and Sir Jean de Clermont discovered they were wearing the emblem of the same woman.

In 1186 the writer Andreas Capellanus listed 31 laws of love. In 1400 the ladies of France, led by Christine de Pisan, set up a Court of Love. It heard cases such as that of a lady who had asked a knight to wear her emblem, then had not attended the tournament.

A lady ties her scarf to her knight's arm and he vows to fight for her in the tournament. The motto on her tent reads: 'Jealousy is the enemy of honour.'

Making Armour

By the fourteenth century armour was made to fit each knight individually. All the different processes were carried out by specialists: hammerers, mailmakers, millmen (polishers), locksmiths (who attached the hinges) and engravers and etchers (who decorated the armour with designs and patterns).

The best armourers, from Germany and northern Italy, sold their armour all over Europe through a network of agents and merchants. They stamped their family emblem

on the steel to show that it was authentic. In the fifteenth century Petrajolo Missaglia of Milan sometimes added an appropriate quotation from the Bible, such as 'Jesus passed safely through the crowd'. Less skilled smiths from local villages forged his mark and sold their imitations as genuine Missaglia armour.

Well-made armour was almost indestructible. It might get battered – you could tell a knight by his misshapen nose – but it could usually be hammered out. Every army took along a portable forge for running repairs. During one tournament, friends of the English knight William Marshall (1144-1219) found him lying with his head on a blacksmith's anvil while the blacksmith hammered at it – a heavy blow had trapped his head inside his helmet.

A nobleman examines the plate armour he is having made (below), while a hammerer beats out the plates from billets of steel forged in the smithy and a master armourer beats a helmet into shape.

A mailmaker (below right and inset left) rivets circlets of wire together into interlocking rings. He works to a pattern, counting the rings in the same way as a knitter counts the number of stitches. In each completed coat of mail he inserts a single ring of brass, stamped with his name.

Arming the Knight

It took about an hour for a squire, sometimes assisted by another servant, to put a harness (a complete suit) of plate armour on a knight. Under the armour the knight wore a padded doublet lined with satin and a pair of worsted trousers called hose. Strips of blanket were tied round his knees to stop the armour rubbing.

Having put the sabatons (shoes) on the knight, the squire clips the greaves around his calves. The cuisses are buckled onto the upper leg with leather straps (inset, right).

Next, the mail skirt is tied to the points – the laces which hang from the doublet (inset, far right). Then comes the padded breastplate and backplate, followed by the vambraces and gauntlets to protect the arms and hands.

Finally, the squire gives the knight his helm and jousting shield.

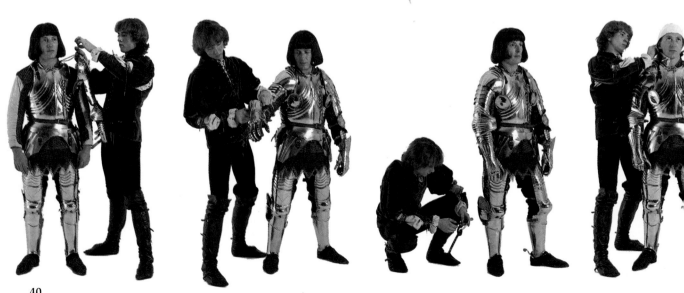

Weapons and White Armour

Improvements in metal-making during the fifteenth century allowed armourers to make stronger steel plate armour (white armour). Its strength was tested by shooting a crossbow at it. The suits weighed about 55 pounds (25 kilograms) but were cleverly jointed to allow the knight to move about easily. Knights never had to be winched into the saddle and could get up if they fell. Young knights sometimes danced in their armour to become familiar with it, and turned somersaults to show off.

Left, a knight in armour. A padded cap makes the sallet (helmet) more comfortable. The vizor is raised. Long hair gives extra comfort, which may explain why this style is fashionable in the fifteenth century.

A bevor (from the French word meaning 'to dribble') protects his chin.

The shield carries the knight's coat of arms, so that other knights will recognize him in battle.

Vambraces – pauldrons (shoulder plates), couters (elbow plates) and cannons (on the upper and lower arm) – protect the knight's arms. Steel discs called besagews protect his armpits when he raises his sword. These parts are joined together with leather, so that he can move his arms easily.

Tassets, and a flexible skirt of mail, protect his hips. The cuisses, poleyns and greaves protect his thighs, kneecaps and calves. Sabatons are shoes made of mail.

The spurs are the sign of knighthood, gained by an act of bravery.

Weapons of the Middle Ages include (right, top to bottom): a buckler (small shield); a falchion (single-edged cutting sword); a war hammer; longbow arrows, including a broad head and two styles of bodkin point; two rondel daggers; a poleaxe; a mace; a shield; a sword; an axe; a hand-and-a-half sword.

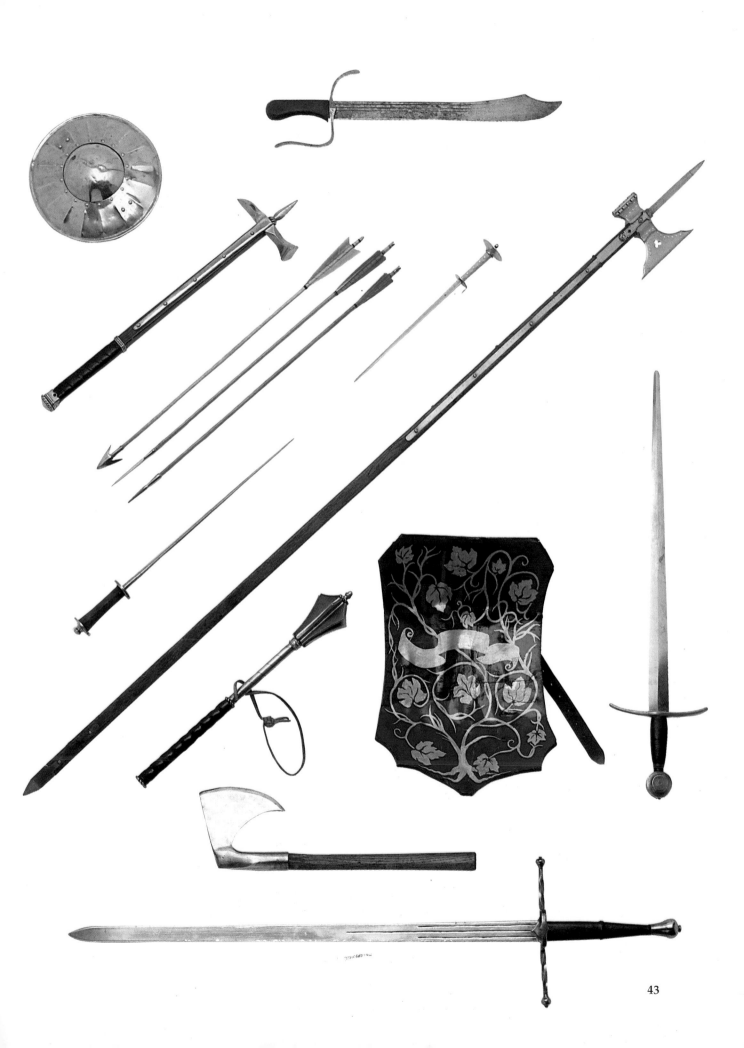

The Siege

A knight did not spend all his life fighting glorious battles. When he was away at war, much of his time was spent besieging castles or towns.

A siege was a long and costly affair, so an army usually tried to take a castle by surprise. More than one castle was captured when a soldier climbed up the sewage chute and lowered the drawbridge.

If surprise failed, the attackers would try to capture the castle by direct assault, using scaling ladders and belfries (siege towers). They pounded the walls with battering rams and hurled rocks weighing up to 300 pounds (136 kilograms) from heavy wooden machines called mangonels and trebuchets. They also threw dead horses and prisoners' heads over the castle walls, to spread disease and alarm.

The defenders, nevertheless, held the advantage. Castle design improved greatly during the Middle Ages and even a large castle could be defended by as few as 60 men-at-arms and 180 archers, who shot at the enemy from towers along the walls. Boiling oil and Greek fire (burning naphtha, a kind of petrol) were poured from hoardings built out over the battlements (see page 27).

The attacking army has decided to mine the castle, so sappers are digging a tunnel under the castle walls. When they have finished, they will burn the props which support the tunnel roof. The unsupported tunnel will collapse, bringing down the wall above. As soon as this happens the attackers will be able to fight their way into the castle through the gap in the defences.

Within the castle walls the garrison build a barricade in the courtyard and wait for the assault.

Starving out the Enemy

If all attempts at assault failed, the attacking army surrounded the town or castle and began to starve it out. Sometimes they built a rival castle called a *malvoisin* (bad neighbour) nearby. In the worst cases – such as at Rouen in 1419 – those trapped in the city became so hungry they ate dogs and rats, and starved their children to save their own lives.

The garrison expelled the useless mouths (people unable to fight); the attacking army refused to let them leave. At Calais in 1346, five hundred women and children were caught between the English and French armies, and so starved to death.

Camping outside the walls, the soldiers suffered from heat, flies and dysentery. As many knights died from disease as in battle in the Middle Ages.

During a long siege the knights grew restless. To relieve their frustration they hanged prisoners in front of the castle walls. The inhabitants retaliated with surprise attacks. In 1351, during a siege at Ploërmel in Brittany, 30 English and 30 French knights fought a battle to the death. The survivors became heroes.

The exasperation of the siege explains why, after a city had fallen, the knights so often massacred the citizens. At the start of a siege a town was called upon to surrender. If this was refused, it was believed, the conquering army had the right to kill all the inhabitants.

During a siege, tents have to be provided for heralds, minstrels, surgeons and a host of workmen, as well as for the thousands of soldiers. This fifteenth-century Burgundian knight waits with the other members of his unit – the men with whom he campaigns. The ingredients of the stew that the servant is making have been pillaged from the local peasants.

Fighting on Horseback

A massed force of knights charging on horseback formed the elite corps of every medieval army. 'The horse and lance are the most dangerous weapons in the world, because they are unstoppable,' wrote Jean de Bueil, a fifteenth-century knight.

Yet knights had few chances to fight in a major battle. Most campaigns aimed to damage the enemy's economy by destroying the countryside, without becoming bogged down in a long siege. The scouts and the incendiaries attacked villages and set fire to the buildings. The role of the cavalry was simply to chase and cut down the fleeing villagers. In warfare such as this the knight in armour was invincible – 'a terrible worm in an iron cocoon,' wrote one eyewitness.

Full-scale battles were rare. In most campaigns knights fought other knights only in skirmishes (minor conflicts involving small numbers) when hostile scouting parties met by chance. Large armies were difficult to manoeuvre and, having drawn close, often wandered apart by accident. Before the Battle of Poitiers in 1356, King Jean of

France had no idea where the English army was positioned, even though it was only a few miles away. He searched in entirely the wrong direction until the English scouts, against orders, attacked the French rear. Most battles were arranged, the commanders agreeing to meet at a certain place at a certain time.

Given the chance to fight in a major battle, the knights were almost uncontrollable. Jean Froissart, a Frenchman who wrote an account of the Hundred Years' War between England and France (1337-1453), complained that 'the commanders could not stop them attacking; they were too eager'. Grouped into disorderly units called *bannières*, knights fought as if they were at a tournament. At Poitiers the senior French knights insisted on riding in the first cavalry charge. Wallowing through the mud into a hail of arrows, the French lost all three of their military commanders in the opening moments of the battle.

Two hostile scouting parties clash in a small skirmish before a battle. The knights deliver huge swinging blows with their swords.

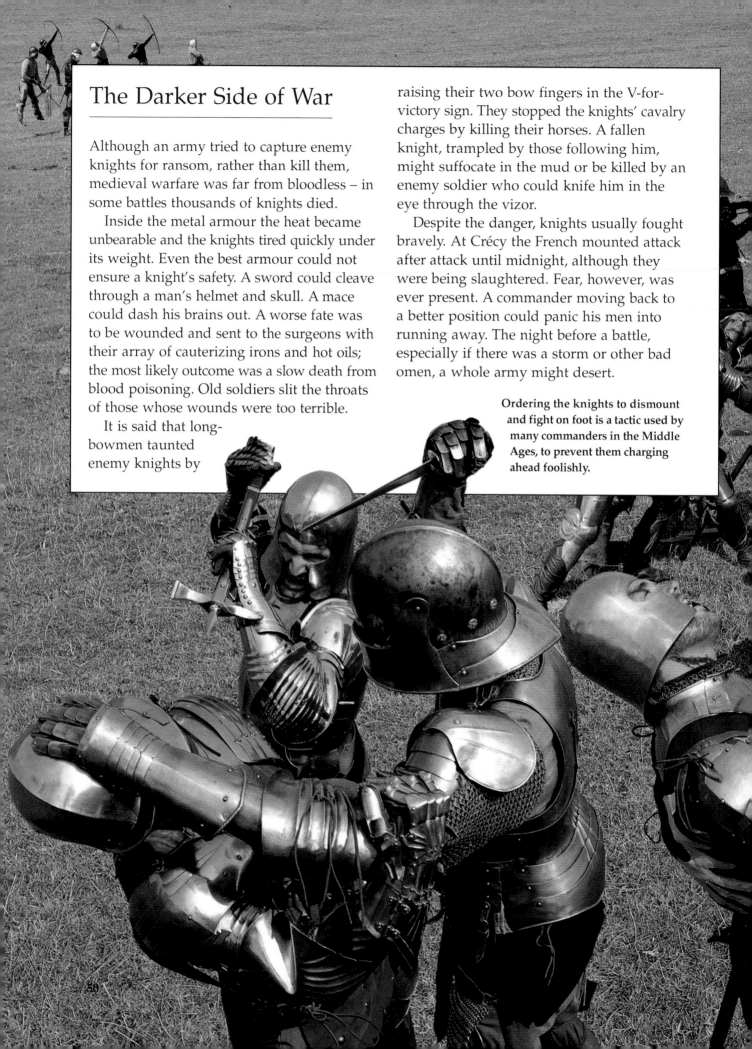

The Darker Side of War

Although an army tried to capture enemy knights for ransom, rather than kill them, medieval warfare was far from bloodless – in some battles thousands of knights died.

Inside the metal armour the heat became unbearable and the knights tired quickly under its weight. Even the best armour could not ensure a knight's safety. A sword could cleave through a man's helmet and skull. A mace could dash his brains out. A worse fate was to be wounded and sent to the surgeons with their array of cauterizing irons and hot oils; the most likely outcome was a slow death from blood poisoning. Old soldiers slit the throats of those whose wounds were too terrible.

It is said that long-bowmen taunted enemy knights by raising their two bow fingers in the V-for-victory sign. They stopped the knights' cavalry charges by killing their horses. A fallen knight, trampled by those following him, might suffocate in the mud or be killed by an enemy soldier who could knife him in the eye through the vizor.

Despite the danger, knights usually fought bravely. At Crécy the French mounted attack after attack until midnight, although they were being slaughtered. Fear, however, was ever present. A commander moving back to a better position could panic his men into running away. The night before a battle, especially if there was a storm or other bad omen, a whole army might desert.

Ordering the knights to dismount and fight on foot is a tactic used by many commanders in the Middle Ages, to prevent them charging ahead foolishly.

The Chase

Between the battles and tournaments knights loved to go hunting. When Edward III of England invaded France in 1346 he took with him 30 falconers and 60 pairs of dogs. On his deathbed, Louis XI of France ordered his servants to release cats and mice in his bedroom so he could still enjoy the thrill of the chase.

Large areas of forest were reserved for hunting and trespassers were severely punished. In France, a nobleman hanged three young knights for hunting on his land. In England, the Bishop of Ely excommunicated a thief who stole his favourite falcon.

The first specialized breeds of dog were developed for hunting: the lymer (similar to a bloodhound), the gazehound (greyhound) and the alaunt (wolfhound). Hunting dogs were kept in large paved kennels, which were heated by fires and faced south. The dogs were given clean straw every day; they had better living conditions than most ordinary people.

Foxes, deer, hares, otters, badgers and conies (rabbits) were all hunted and killed.

Wolves were lured into traps and beaten to death with sticks. Most of all, the knights loved to hunt the boar, on horseback, with a long, broad, sharp spear. 'He is more formidable than an armed man,' commented a medieval writer.

A knight goes hawking with his lady, who rides side-saddle. The falconer, who has trained from childhood, wears a wooden frame on which he carries the birds. The jesses (leather straps) which are attached to the birds' legs are used to stop them escaping. When prey is spotted the falconer will select one of the birds, remove its hood and release it.

The Tournament

In the tournaments of the early Middle Ages knights formed teams and tried to capture each other. This type of tournament was called a melee.

Often, the knights were so carried away by all the excitement that they refused to stop when ordered. Their squires joined in and the tournament became a real battle. When Edward I of England captured a French knight at a melee in 1273, the French attacked so furiously that the tournament became known as the Little War of Chalons. The war-like knight of the early Middle Ages liked to 'see his blood flow and hear his teeth crack'. Sometimes he fought *à outrance* (to the death). The tournament was a training for war.

After about 1400, however, tournaments changed. Pageantry and play-acting increased. Stands, beautifully decorated with the coats of arms of the competitors, were erected for spectators. Knights organized events called *pas d'armes*, challenging other knights to joust with them. They pretended to defend a maiden in her castle or to rescue a lady from an evil giant. Tournaments became opportunities to show off to the ladies and indulge in courtly love.

By the end of the Middle Ages tournaments were beginning to go out of fashion. At a *pas d'armes* at St Omer in France only one middle-aged German knight turned up.

In a joust two knights charge at one another. Each man tries to break his lance on his opponent's shield. They score points for the number of lances broken. Wearing heavy armour to protect them from accidental injury, they fight *à plaisaunce*   (for pleasure) with blunted or capped weapons.   For additional safety, they joust 'at the   barriers' with a wooden fence   between them.

54

The Professional Soldier

The first knights were warriors, who were given land in return for their services to the king. As one generation succeeded another, however, the knights became less warlike. Soldiering was uncomfortable and dangerous. They preferred to stay at home on their estates, feasting, dancing and playing dice and chess. Their sons studied law and were given jobs in the government. When Edward I called out the English feudal army in 1277, only 377 knights reported for duty.

It became necessary for kings to employ mercenaries – soldiers who signed a contract to fight and were paid a wage. In the English army in the fourteenth century, for example, a man serving as a knight received two shillings a day. In 1366 one shilling bought six pairs of gloves or one hundred herrings.

These paid soldiers were reliable in battle,

but when a war ended they were left with nothing to do. During lulls in the fighting in the Hundred Years' War, huge gangs of mercenaries, called the Free Companies, wandered around France, robbing the peasants and burning the crops.

They caused so much trouble that in 1439 Charles VII decided he would have to employ some of them on a full-time basis. He hired one group as a permanent army and used it to destroy the others. The days of the feudal army were over; the age of the professional soldier had begun.

In Italy, condottieri (from the Italian word *condota*, meaning contract) sell their services to the highest bidder. Towns pay the men to fight for them – then pay them to go and pillage elsewhere.

The mercenaries are not interested in glory. They want to live to enjoy their earnings, so they work out less reckless tactics than those used by the knights earlier in the Middle Ages. The aim of their tactics is to win the battle with as few casualties as possible.

Gunpowder

Gunpowder was invented in China before AD 1000. In Europe it was called Chinese snow. Medieval writers thought that it was invented by evil magicians, helped by the devil.

The Italians were the first people to use gunpowder to fire missiles. In about 1330 they produced new weapons called thunder tubes (the word cannon comes from the Latin *canna*, meaning tube). They were made of strips of metal welded together. In France, in 1375, it took 13 smiths, three forges and 2,300 pounds (1,040 kilograms) of iron to build one cannon. Although metal rings were welded round the barrel to stop it bursting, King James I of Scotland was killed at the test-firing of a cannon in 1437 when the barrel exploded.

Large cannons, which were made of wrought iron, were called bombards, from the Greek word for a loud humming noise. The English named their cannons after popular heroes such as Robin Hood. The French had one called The Greatest in the World.

Artillery design improved rapidly. At Bordeaux in 1420 an English cannon fired a stone cannonball weighing 784 pounds (356 kilograms). By the sixteenth century bronze cannons were at last able to hurl a missile further than the range of a longbow.

The cannon changed siege warfare completely, reducing the length of a siege from over a year to a few months. Towns tried unsuccessfully to protect their walls by building mounds of earth in front of them. After 1450 every army had experienced *cannoneurs*, who built trenches around the enemy town or castle and directed the bombardment.

Cannoneurs bombard the castle. Left, top to bottom: they pack gunpowder into the barrel, load the stone cannonball, then light a small charge of gunpowder above a hole in the barrel. A spark travels through the hole to ignite the main charge.

The New Knights

In the early Middle Ages the knight was a fighting machine. He was violent, sometimes cruel and often uneducated.

Gradually, however, the knights came to believe in love and chivalry. They lost battles because of their desire for glory. By the end of the Middle Ages the cannon and the handgun had replaced them as the supreme fighting force. Knights, who had held a high position in society because they were warriors, could no longer win battles. When they fell from their horses, they were killed.

Foot soldiers stole their armour then looted their baggage, cutting and slashing the clothes to make them fit.

Kings had to hire full-time, professional soldiers. Some knights still joined cavalry units, but by the sixteenth century they fought in disciplined groups called lances, with a number of handgunners or pikemen. They were used to attack the enemy or to chase enemy soldiers who ran away. If the attack failed, the riders fell back and regrouped behind the pikes.

Knights, in general, ceased to be warriors. In France, merchants bought knighthoods, because knights did not have to pay taxes. A

middle-class French knight would put on his sword each morning and walk proudly past his warehouse. Tournaments, which had been violent conflicts, became ridiculous pageants. At the *pas d'armes* put on for the wedding of Charles the Bold in 1468, a female dwarf rode in on a mechanical lion, and a life-sized model whale sang and wiggled its tail. Nobles wore multicoloured 'slashed' clothes in imitation of the Swiss footsoldiers, but they wore them for dancing, not fighting.

In 1605 the Spanish writer Cervantes tried to show that knights were not needed any more. In his book *Don Quixote*, a tired old knight wanders about the countryside, charging at windmills (the 'enemy') for the sake of a 'lady' who is really just a peasant girl. His 'silly ideals of knight errantry' make him look foolish.

The knight in shining armour disappeared from history, but his ideals of courtesy and honour lived on. They are still the civilizing forces of society.

The pikemen have taken up a pointed hedgehog formation, with the bravest soldiers in front. Behind the pikes the handgunners reload. In the distance the knights prepare to charge. By the sixteenth century, however, a well-ordered unit of pikemen is virtually invulnerable to a cavalry charge.

How Do We Know?

There is a great deal of evidence about the knights and their world. The problem is to decide how much of it can be believed.

Literary sources

Many books were written about knighthood and chivalry in the Middle Ages, including *The Art of Courtly Love* (1186) by Andreas Capellanus, *The Book of the Order of Chyvalrie* (1265) by Raimon Llull, and *Le Jouvencel* by the fifteenth-century writer Jean de Bueil. Other writers described the events of the time. One of the most reliable and informative chroniclers was a Frenchman called Jean Froissart (1337-1410), who wrote a history of the Hundred Years' War. His account is full of stories about the knights, some of which appear in this book.

Reading and writing, however, was mainly taught in the monasteries in the Middle Ages, so most writers of the time were churchmen – the surname Capellanus, for example, means chaplain. It is not surprising, therefore, that some of their writings were biased. Many churchmen hated the warlike knights. If they did not already know some unpleasant gossip about a man they disliked, they

simply made it up. Reading the books of the period one could be forgiven for thinking that in the Middle Ages the Church was all-powerful, the women were weak, and all the knights were brutal.

Other documents have survived from the Middle Ages. Many nobles – for instance, the Paston family in England – kept records of their estates, and much of their correspondence. Historians studying the Middle Ages can read thousands of royal writs (written orders), financial transactions and records of court cases. These often provide fascinating

details of everyday life. At the same time they must be used carefully. A history written just from court cases, for instance, would make any society look violent and criminal.

To add to his knowledge the historian can read wonderful stories such as the medieval romances and the *Chansons de Geste,* Chaucer's *Canterbury Tales* and Cervantes' *Don Quixote*. These writings can be helpful as they were often based on real life, but it is important to remember that they are works of fiction.

Other sources

There are several other ways of finding out about the knights. For instance, they were

often wealthy enough to have valuable possessions, some of which have survived. Many of their castles still stand. Historians can peer through an arrow slit, or climb down into the oubliette where prisoners were thrown and forgotten. You can sit on a knight's chair, handle his weapons or wear his armour.

Tapestries dating from the Middle Ages show knights in battle and out hunting. Although the paintings of the time were mainly religious, the artists dressed the Bible characters in medieval clothes and armour and showed them living in medieval towns.

Into modern times

After Cervantes, chivalry was forgotten until the nineteenth century, when Sir Walter Scott wrote his great romantic novel *Ivanhoe* (1819). Knights and chivalry came back into fashion. In 1839 the Earl of Eglington, a rich young English lord, held a full-scale tournament, with pavilions, horses and costumes.

Early in the twentieth century Hollywood discovered the Middle Ages and the tales of the knights in armour were told on celluloid. The film-makers, however, were no more

interested in the truth than the people of the Middle Ages had been. In their stories all the good knights were gentle and brave and all the bad knights were evil.

Modern historians have found out that knights did not really hunt for the Holy Grail, or rescue their ladies on white chargers. Yet, in every one of us, there is something that thrills to the idea of the knight in armour riding out for God and for valour.

Index

Accolade The blow by which a man became a knight, 32
Agriculture 13, 14-15, 17
Andreas Capellanus Author, 37, 62
Armour 7, 8, 13, 25, 27, 34-5, 37, 38-9, 40, 42, 48, 50, 60-1, 63
Arrière-ban Call-to-arms of the knights, 13, 56
Atrocities Vicious actions, 7, 15, 18, 22, 24, 27, 45, 47, 50, 57

Bannières Groups of knights in battle, 49
Barons Tenants-in-chief of the king, 13, 14; see also **Fief**
Blacksmith 13, 39, 58
Bombards A type of **cannon**, 58
Byzantium 21, 22, 25

Cannoneurs 58
Cannons Medieval artillery, 58
Castles 14, 18, 27, 45, 47, 58, 63
Cavalry 7, 13, 48-9, 50, 60
Chansons de geste Songs about the deeds of Charlemagne, 34, 62
Charles VII King of France (1422-1461), 57
Children 7, 27, 28, 30-1, 32, 47, 53
China 7, 58
Chivalry The knight's code of behaviour, see **Ideals**
Christine de Pisan Writer (1364-1430), 27, 37
Combat of the Thirty An event in the **Hundred Years' War**, 47
Compostela A place of **pilgrimage** in northern Spain, 18
Condottieri **Mercenaries**, 57
Court baron The manor court, 15
Courtly love 31, 35, 37, 54; see also **Ideals**
Crécy Site of a battle in the **Hundred Years' War**, 50
Crusades Wars to win the **Holy Land** from the **Muslims**, 20-5, 27

Don Quixote Fictional **knight errant** in a book written by Miguel de Cervantes, 61, 62

Edward I King of **England** (1272-1307), 27, 54, 56
Edward III King of **England** (1327-1377), 52

England 7, 11, 13, 27, 28, 32, 34, 37, 47, 49, 52, 54, 56, 58
Entertainment 6, 11, 15, 22-3, 28, 30-1, 34-5, 47, 52-3, 54, 56

Fief Land granted by a king to **barons** and knights, 13, 14-15, 23
France 6, 7, 14, 15, 16, 18, 21, 27, 32, 37, 47, 49, 50, 52, 54, 57, 58
Free Companies Groups of unemployed **mercenaries**, 57

Geoffrey Chaucer English poet (1340-1400), 18, 62
Germany 22, 35, 38, 54
Gunpowder 58

Hawking 13, 53
Henry II King of England (1154-1189), 11, 27
Holy Land 18, 20-5
Hundred Years' War War between **France** and **England** (1337-1453), 37, 47, 48, 49, 50, 52, 57, 58
Hunting 52-3, 63

Ideals 7, 13, 16-17, 18, 20, 22-3, 24-5, 32, 34-5, 37, 49, 50, 54, 63
Infantry 8, 50, 60-1
Italy 7, 18, 21, 35, 38-9, 57, 58

James I King of Scotland, 58
Jean II King of France (1350-1364), 37, 48
Jean de Bueil Writer and knight (1405-1478), 48, 62
Jean Froissart Chronicler (1337-1410) of the **Hundred Years' War**, 49, 62
Jerusalem see **Holy Land**
Jongleurs Knights who travelled round singing the *chansons de geste*, 37
Jousts See **Tournaments**

Knights errant Knights seeking adventure or travelling to **tournaments**, 34-5, 61

Law of Arms 37; see also **Ideals**
Little War of Chalons A very violent **tournament** (1273), 54
Longbowmen 49, 50
Louis XI King of France (1461-1483), 52

Malvoisin A siege tower, 47
Manor See **Fief**

Medicine 6-7, 11, 18, 47, 50
Melee See **Tournaments**
Mercenaries Paid soldiers, 56-7, 58
Minstrels See **Jongleurs**
Muslims 7, 20-1, 22, 24-5

Page A child, 7-14 years old, training to be a knight, 30-1
Pas d'armes A **tournament**, 54, 61
Paston family 28, 62
Pikemen 60-1
Pilgrimage 18, 20
Pillory Minor criminals were put here as punishment, 15
Poitiers Site of a battle between **England** and **France** in the **Hundred Years' War**, 37, 48-9
Pope Head of the Roman Catholic Church, 6, 7, 16, 21, 22

Raimon Llull Traveller, writer, missionary and knight, 7, 37, 62
Religion 6-7, 16-17, 18, 20-1, 22-3, 28, 30, 31, 32, 34, 39, 52, 58, 62
Richard the Lionheart King of England, 24

Sieges 27, 45, 47, 58
Solar Women's sitting room, 28
Spain 7, 18, 37
Squire A knight's attendant, or a man training to be a knight, 30-1, 32, 35, 40, 54

Templars This Order of Knights protected people on **pilgrimage** in the **Holy Land**, 18, 22-3, 24
Tithes One tenth of all produce, demanded by the Church, 16-17
Tournaments 35, 37, 39, 54, 61, 63
Towns 6-7, 47, 57, 58
Truce of God The Church forbade warfare on Sundays, 16, 37

Ulrich von Lichtenstein Famous jouster and knight errant, 35
Urban II The **pope** who inspired the **crusades**, 21, 22

Villeins The peasants, 6, 13, 14-15, 17, 22, 47, 48, 57

Warhorses 7, 13, 23, 31, 35, 48-9, 63
Weapons 42, 50, 54, 58, 63
William Marshall Famous English knight, 39
Women 14, 27-8, 30-1, 32, 34-5, 37, 47, 53, 54, 61

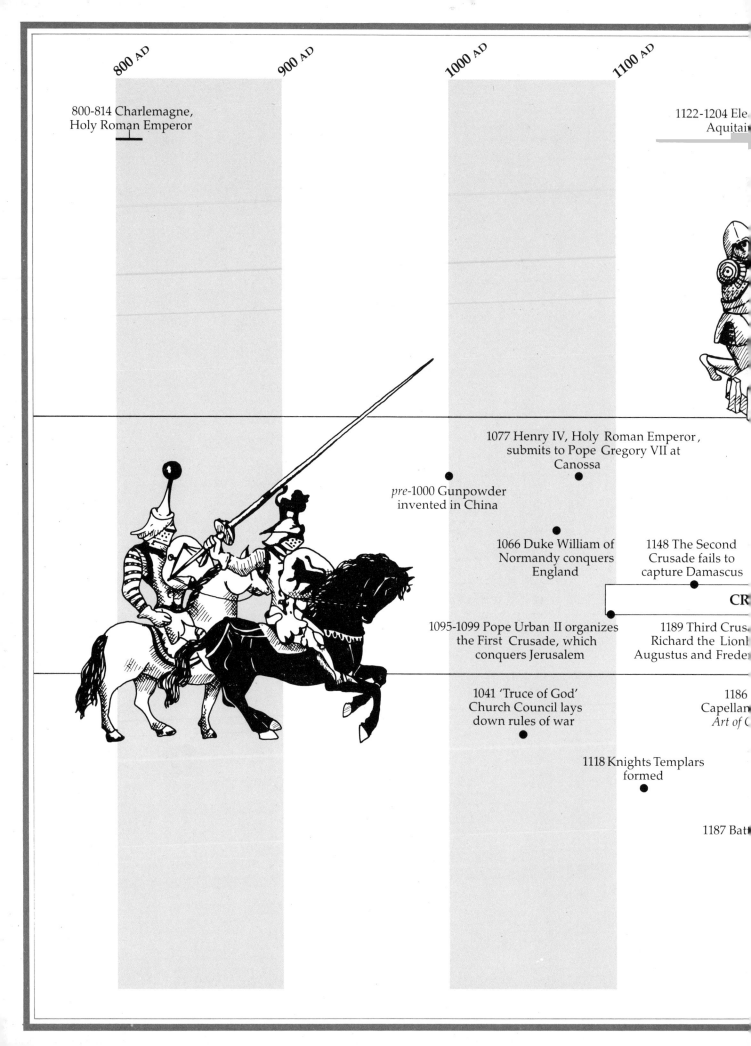

800 AD   900 AD   1000 AD   1100 AD

800-814 Charlemagne,
Holy Roman Emperor

1122-1204 Ele
Aquitai

1077 Henry IV, Holy Roman Emperor,
submits to Pope Gregory VII at
Canossa

pre-1000 Gunpowder
invented in China

1066 Duke William of
Normandy conquers
England

1148 The Second
Crusade fails to
capture Damascus

CR

1095-1099 Pope Urban II organizes
the First Crusade, which
conquers Jerusalem

1189 Third Crus
Richard the Lionh
Augustus and Frede

1041 'Truce of God'
Church Council lays
down rules of war

1186
Capellan
Art of C

1118 Knights Templars
formed

1187 Bat